HEREFORDSHIRE
AND
WORCESTERSHIRE
COUNTRY RECIPES

COMPILED BY
MOLLY PERHAM

℞℞
RAVETTE BOOKS

Published by Ravette Books Limited
3 Glenside Estate, Star Road
Partridge Green, Horsham,
West Sussex RH13 8RA
(0403) 710392

Production: Oval Projects Ltd.
Cover design: Jim Wire
Typesetting: Repro-type
Printing & binding: Norhaven A/S

All recipes are given in Imperial and Metric
weights and measures. Where measurements
are given in 'cups', these are American cups,
holding 8 fluid ounces.

The recipes contained in this book are traditional
and many have been compiled from archival sources.
Every effort has been made to ensure that the recipes
are correct.

RECITES

HEREFORDSHIRE AND WORCESTERSHIRE

Herefordshire and Worcestershire, at the heart of England, is a fertile region with a warm climate from the Gulf Stream. The rich, heavy soil is ideal for apple orchards, and all kinds are grown - not only cooking and eating varieties, but many cider apples as well. The area around Hereford is especially good for cider, and the large cider-makers Bulmers is based here. 'Scrumpy' — the true cider that is so strong the smell alone can make the head spin — is still produced in small quantities on some of the farms, though it is difficult to find in the pubs.

Until the 17th century cider was made from crab apples. Then Lord Scudamore, a man who devoted his life to the making of cider, started to experiment with growing trees scientifically. His estate at Kentchurch in Herefordshire was turned over to apple orchards, and after years of work he produced the most famous redstreak cider apple of its day, the Scudamore's Arab.

The time for cider-making is late autumn, between September and Christmas. On January 6th an old custom was to take the Wassail Bowl full of cider round the cow byre to toast the cattle, while a cake with a hole through the centre was hung on the horns of an ox. If it was tossed backwards it went to the mistress of the house, and if forwards it went to the bailiff or headman. A large plum cake was also made. This had a bean in it, and the person who got the slice of cake containing the bean was king for the day. The apple orchards were blessed on St. Peter's Day and St. Swithin's Day. It was said in Herefordshire that they must be blessed on St. Peter's Day or there would be a poor crop.

The traditional method of making cider in Herefordshire was to crush the apples between heavy stone wheels. A horse was harnessed to one of the wheels, and it plodded slowly round the mill as the apples were loaded. The resulting pulp was then packed into thick horsehair mats that were set into a screw press made of iron or stone. The juice ran out into barrels or vats. Three hundred years ago Lord Scudamore started the idea of putting cider into heavy glass wine bottles that were strong enough to resist bursting and the jolts of the long road journey.

Today, fizzy, sweet, and golden bottled cider is big business. In recent years cider-makers have discovered those large trees with twisted, tangled branches took up too much room and were inconvenient for picking, so they have been replaced with squat, bushlike trees that produce a heavier crop in a smaller space.

Pears also grow well in the area. Conference and Comice for eating and cooking, as well as the famous perry pears. Perry is the fermented juice from certain varieties of pear that were introduced into the country about the time of the Norman Conquest. They are less 'pear-shaped' than eating varieties, and their names date back hundreds of years - Yellow Huffcap, Thorn Pear, and Red Pear, which looks more like a ripe red apple. Unlike cider, perry is not blended but made from the juice of a single variety.

Beer is also produced in Herefordshire and Worcestershire. Next to Kent, this is the most important hop-growing area in the country, and hop fields are a common sight throughout the region. The beer brewed at Penrhos Court in Herefordshire is very clean-tasting, thin, and deceptively mild.

Other fruit grown in the area are plums — particularly the Pershore variety — and in the Vale of Evesham strawberries, cherries, blackberries, gooseberries, raspberries, blackcurrants and redcurrants. The Vale of Evesham is famous for its asparagus, too. Indeed it is one of the main areas where asparagus is grown. The thin stems of Worcestershire asparagus are easily distinguishable from the fat green asparagus grown in Norfolk, Suffolk and Essex.

Vegetables grown in Herefordshire and Worcestershire include tomatoes, lettuces, cabbages, potatoes, sprouts, turnips and peas. In the early part of the 18th century a Herefordshire squire called Thomas Andrew Knight was the first to raise plants by cross-fertilization. He introduced the first wrinkled pea, which was named the Marrow Pea.

Hereford is famous for its cattle, which produces some of the best beef in the country. Because the soil tends to be heavy it is better for grazing and pasture than arable farming. Hereford cattle, with their white faces, red markings and down-pointing horns, are a common sight in the meadows.

The rivers Wye and Severn, which cut through Worcestershire, produce an abundance of salmon, eels, and other fish. Worcestershire is also famous for its sauce.

Prime beef, salmon, fresh fruit and vegetables — all washed down with local cider, perry or beer — form the basis of Hereford and Worcester eating at its best.

'Herefordshire, a county that hath the best in wool, the best of cider, the best of fruit, the best of wheat, and the best rivers.'

Andrew Yarrenton, 1677

'Then hey for covert and woodland,
And ash, and elm and oak,
Tewkesbury inns and Malvern roofs,
and Worcestershire chimney smoke.'

John Masefield

HERB SOUP

This recipe comes from an 18th century Worcestershire cook.

A knuckle of veal
Half a neck of mutton
8 oz (225 g) brisket of beef
Some lettuce leaves
A handful of sorrel
An endive
2 onions
1 tablespoon chopped herbs — sweet marjoram, sage or
   rosemary
¼ teaspoon ground cloves
¼ teaspoon mace
A ham bone
Some asparagus tops

Put the knuckle of veal, neck of mutton and brisket of beef into a large saucepan.

Cover with cold water.

Bring to boil and simmer gently for 7 hours.

From time to time skim off any scum that rises to the surface.

Add the lettuce leaves, sorrel, endive, chopped onions, herbs, cloves, mace and the ham bone.

Boil quickly for 30 minutes.

Strain, and return the broth to the saucepan.

Add the asparagus tops and let the soup boil for a further 10 minutes.

Serve hot.

CREAMED ASPARAGUS SOUP

Serves 8

This popular summer soup can be made from tough asparagus stalks and trimmings.

1 lb (450 g) asparagus stalks and trimmings
3 oz (75 g) butter
3 oz (75 g) flour
1 pint (600 ml/ 2½ cups) milk
2 pints (1.15 litres/ 5 cups) chicken stock
A bouquet garni
1 tablespoon sugar
Salt and pepper
¼ pint (150 ml/ ⅔ cup) double cream
2 egg yolks
Cooked asparagus tips to garnish

Cut the asparagus into small pieces and put in a heavy-based pan with the butter.

Cover with a lid and simmer gently until the asparagus is golden.

Stir in the flour.

Gradually add the milk and stock, stirring continuously to prevent lumps forming.

Add the bouquet garni and sugar.

Season with salt and pepper.

Bring to the boil and simmer for 1 hour.

Blend in a liquidizer or rub through a sieve.

Blend the cream and egg yolks together and add to the soup.

Reheat, but do not allow to boil.

Garnish with asparagus tips before serving.

THE JUDGE'S CIRCUIT SOUP

This soup was served at a dinner at the Town Hall for the Corporation of Worcester in the early 18th century.

The knuckle and lean part of a leg of veal
6 cloves
A pinch of mace
Black and white pepper
4 oz (100 g) rice
2 pints (1.15 litres/ 5 cups) water

Break the bones of the leg of veal and cut up the meat.

Put into a large saucepan and cover with water.

Add the cloves, mace, and some black and white pepper.

Bring to the boil and simmer gently for 2-3 hours.

From time to time skim off any scum that rises to the surface.

Boil the rice in the 2 pints of water until the water has gone.

Strain the soup and thicken it with the rice.

Season to taste.

Serve hot.

TOMATO SOUP

1 onion
2 tablespoons oil
1 lb (675 g) tomatoes
1 bay leaf
½ level teaspoon dried marjoram
½ level teaspoon salt
Pepper
1 level teaspoon sugar
1 pint (600 ml/ 2 cups) stock

Peel the onion and slice thinly.

Heat the oil in a saucepan and gently fry the onion until soft but not brown.

Skin and chop the tomatoes.

Add to the saucepan with the bay leaf, marjoram, salt, pepper and sugar.

Stir in the stock.

Bring to the boil and simmer gently for 25 minutes, or until the vegetables are cooked.

Sieve or blend until smooth.

Reheat before serving.

SORREL SOUP

On the acid soil of west Herefordshire sorrel grows wild in the meadows.

8 oz (225 g) sorrel leaves
1 oz (25 g) buter
½ oz (15 g) plain flour
2 pints (1.15 litres/ 5 cups) boiling stock or water

Remove the tough centre stalk and any damaged leaves.

Melt the butter in a saucepan and cook the sorrel leaves for about 20 minutes.

Stir in the flour and cook gently for another 2 minutes.

Add the boiling stock or water gradually, stirring well to avoid lumps.

Season with the salt and sugar.

Cover the pan and simmer gently for 15 minutes.

Mix a little of the hot soup with the beaten egg, then add to the pan, but do not allow to boil.

Stir well to thicken.

Serve hot.

COUNTRY PATÉ

8 oz (225 g) chicken livers
8 oz (225 g) bacon or fat pork
4 rashers streaky bacon
2 oz (50 g) fresh white breadcrumbs
1 onion
1 clove of garlic
2 eggs
1 tablespoon sherry or brandy
Salt and pepper
3 bay leaves
1 oz (25 g) butter

Mince the chicken livers and bacon or fat pork.

Add the breadcrumbs, chopped onion and garlic, and mince again.

Stir in the beaten egg and sherry or brandy.

Season well with salt and pepper.

Line an ovenproof dish with the rashers of bacon.

Spoon in the meat mixture.

Arrange the bay leaves on top.

Stand the dish in a meat tin and add about 1 inch (2.5 cm) of water.

Bake in a moderate oven for 1½ hours.

Leave to cool.

Melt the butter in a saucepan and pour over the top.

Serve cold, with toast.

SALMON MOUSSE

This will serve four people for lunch, with a salad, or eight as a starter to dinner.

1 fresh salmon
1 oz (25 g) gelatine
1 tablespoon sherry
Salt and pepper
2 egg whites

Put the salmon into a saucepan and cover with the water.

Poach gently until the flesh comes away from the bone.

Lift the salmon out of the pan and reserve the fish stock.

Remove all skin and bones and leave to cool.

Dissolve the gelatine in 1 pint (600 ml/ 2½ cups) of the fish stock.

Add the sherry and season to taste.

Leave to cool.

Put the egg whites in a small cup and stand in a saucepan of simmering water. Cook until firm.

Leave to cool and then cut into fancy shapes.

Cover the bottom of a mould with some of the jellied stock and leave to set.

Decorate with the egg white shapes.

Add another layer of jellied stock and leave to set.

Add alternate layers of cooked salmon and jellied stock until the mould is full, finishing with a layer of jelly.

Keep in the refrigerator until ready to serve.

Turn out on to a serving dish and garnish with cucumber slices.

WYE BAKED SALMON

8 salmon steaks weighing approx. 6 oz (175 g) each
12 oz (350 g) shortcrust pastry
2 oz (50 g) fresh white breadcrumbs
2 oz (50 g) chopped mushrooms
2 oz (50 g) melted butter
4 oz (100 g) cooked, flaked salmon
4 oz (100 g) cooked, flaked eel
¼ teaspoon grated nutmeg
¼ teaspoon ground cloves
Salt and pepper
2 eggs
Milk
8 oysters
2 tablespoons red wine
Juice of 1 lemon

Line a 3 pint (1.75 litre) pie dish with pastry.

Leave the salmon steaks in boiling water for a few minutes.

Drain and remove the skin.

Cook the breadcrumbs and mushrooms in 1 oz (15 g) of the butter.

Blend in the cooked, flaked salmon and eel.

Season to taste with nutmeg, cloves, salt and pepper.

Remove from the heat and bind this stuffing with the lightly beaten eggs and a little milk.

Arrange the salmon steaks over the pastry base.

Cover with the stuffing and sprinkle with a few breadcrumbs and a little melted butter.

Place the cleaned oysters around the salmon.

Boil the remaining butter with the wine and lemon juice and pour over the salmon.

Bake in a moderate oven for 45 minutes.

Oven: 350°F/180°C Gas Mark 4

POACHED SALMON

Serves 4

1-1½ lb (450-675 g) piece of salmon
½ pint (300 ml/ 1¼ cups) water
½ teaspoon salt
1 teaspoon tarragon vinegar

Put the salmon into an ovenproof dish.

Add the salt and vinegar to the water.

Pour over the salmon.

Cover the dish with a lid or with aluminium foil.

Bake in a moderately hot oven for about 30 minutes, or until the flesh comes away from the bone.

Serve hot with the cooking juices, or cold with salad.

POTTED WYE SALMON

Serves 8

This recipe for potting salmon from the River Wye dates from the 18th century.

1 large salmon
Salt
¼ teaspoon mace
¼ teaspoon powdered cloves
6 black peppercorns
2 bay leaves
2 oz (50 g) butter
4 oz (100 g) clarified butter

Scale the salmon.

Wipe it clean, but do not wash it.

Place on a dish, salt it well, and leave till the salt melts.

Drain it off and place in a roasting tin.

Add the mace, cloves, peppercorns and bay leaves.

Dot the top with knobs of butter.

Cover with foil.

Bake in a moderate oven, allowing 10 minutes per lb and 10 minutes over.

Lift out and drain the salmon.

Remove the skin and bones.

Pound the flesh and pack it tightly into small pots.

Pour over the clarified butter and leave to set.

Oven: 350°F/180°C Gas Mark 4

GRAYLING IN BEER

Serves 8

Grayling is a member of the salmon and trout family, found in the fast rivers and streams of Herefordshire. It spawns in the spring so is at its best from August to February.

8 grayling
2 pints (1.15 litres/ 5 cups) beer
1 dessertspoon grated horseradish
A sprig each of thyme and winter savory
Salt and pepper
1 oz (15 g) butter
Grated lemon rind
¼ teaspoon ground ginger

Scale and clean the fish, washing them thoroughly.

Make three scores on one side of each fish.

Place the fish in a large saucepan and cover with the beer.

Add most of the horseradish, reserving a little for a garnish.

Add the sprigs of thyme and winter savory.

Season with salt and pepper.

Bring to the boil and simmer until the fish are tender.

Remove from the saucepan and drain.

Arrange on a serving dish and keep warm.

Strain the cooking liquid and measure ½ pint (300 ml) of this into a saucepan.

Add the butter, heat through, and pour over the fish.

Sprinkle with the remaining horseradish, grated lemon rind and ground ginger before serving.

GRILLED GRAYLING

6 good-sized grayling
A bunch of fresh herbs — chervil, chives, tarragon and
   parsley
6 oz (175 g) butter
Salt and pepper

Clean the fish thoroughly.

Make two diagonal slits to the bone on both sides.

Chop the herbs and mix them with the butter.

Season with salt and pepper.

Smear half the butter on the fish and into the cuts.

Put under a hot grill for 4 minutes.

Turn the fish over and spread the rest of the butter in the
other sides.

Grill the other sides for 4 minutes.

Pour the juices from the grill pan over the fish.

Serve immediately.

GRILLED EEL WITH TARTARE SAUCE

Serves 6

Eels are common in the rivers of Herefordshire, but are very hard to catch.
They are also very difficult to skin — so it's best to buy them at the
fishmonger's ready prepared.

3 skinned eels
Salt and pepper
5 tablespoons olive oil
5 tablespoons lemon juice
5 tablespoons wine vinegar

For the tartare sauce:
½ pint (300 ml/ 1¼ cups) mayonnaise
1 teaspoon chopped capers
1 teaspoon chopped chives
1 teaspoon chopped parsley
1 teaspoon chopped gherkins

Put the pieces of eel into a flat dish.

Season well with salt and pepper.

Mix the olive oil, lemon juice and vinegar together to make
a marinade.

Pour over the pieces of eel and leave for 2 hours.

Grill under a moderate heat until the flesh comes away from
the bone.

Place the pieces on a serving dish.

Mix together the ingredients for the tartare sauce.

Serve the sauce with the grilled eel.

STUFFED LAMPREY

Serves 6-8

This scaleless, eel-like fish used to be caught in great numbers in the river Severn in the months of April and May. It was highly prized in the Middle Ages and remained a delicacy until the 19th century. The soft, glutinous flesh has a delicate taste but is difficult to digest. The other reason why it is not as popular now as it once was is that there are two filaments down the back that must be cut out before cooking as they are poisonous.

1 lamprey
Salt
8 oz (225 g) veal forcemeat (see recipe) or parsley
stuffing
2 oz (50 g) lard

Rub the lamprey with plenty of salt to remove any slime.

Wash well in warm water.

Gut the lamprey and remove the head and tail.

Cut out the cartilage and the two filaments on each side.

Fill the belly with veal forcemeat or parsley stuffing.

Roll up the lamprey and tie securely.

Put into a saucepan and cover with water.

Bring the water to the boil and simmer gently for 15 minutes.

Remove the lamprey, drain it and pat dry.

Put into a roasting tin with the lard.

Bake in a moderate oven for about 1 hour, or until the flesh is tender.

Serve with caper sauce.

Oven: 350°F/180°C Gas Mark 4

CIDER CHICKEN

Serves 4

Cider is the local drink and is much used in traditional dishes as the liquid in which meat and poultry is cooked.

4 chicken pieces
Seasoned flour
2 oz (50 g) butter
1 onion
1 oz (25 g) flour
½ pint (300 ml/ 1¼ cups) cider
2 tablespoons tomato purée
A sprig each of parsley, thyme and sage

Remove the skin from the chicken pieces.

Dust with seasoned flour.

Melt half the butter in a frying pan and brown the chicken pieces on both sides.

Remove to a casserole.

Slice the onion and fry gently until soft.

Add to the chicken pieces.

Melt the remaining butter and stir in the flour.

Cook gently for a couple of minutes, then stir in the cider.

Bring slowly to the boil until thickened.

Add the tomato purée and cook for a further 2 minutes.

Pour the sauce over the chicken.

Chop the herbs and add to the casserole.

Cook in a moderate oven for about 1 hour, or until the chicken is tender.

Oven: 350°F/180°C Gas Mark 4

RAISED CHICKEN PIE

Serves 8-10

Originally, the hot water crust pastry for a raised pie was moulded and raised up the sides of the filling by hand. This required great skill as the hot pastry cooled quickly and was liable to crack. It is much easier to make the pie in a tin or pie dish.

1 boiling chicken
1 lb (450 g) plain flour
A pinch of salt
4 oz (100 g) lard
½ pint (300 ml/ 1¼ cups) hot water
6 oz (175 g) bacon
Salt and pepper
Beaten egg for glazing
½ oz (15 g) gelatine

Boil the chicken until the flesh is tender.

Leave to cool.

Remove all the flesh from the bones.

Reserve the stock.

Sift the flour and salt into a warm mixing basin.

Make a well in the centre.

Put the lard into a saucepan with the hot water and boil until the lard is melted.

Pour into the flour and mix quickly with a wooden spoon.

Knead the pastry while it is still warm, until it is smooth and free from cracks.

Reserve a quarter of the pastry for the lid.

Roll out the rest to line a tin or pie dish — this must be done before the pastry hardens.

Cut the bacon into small chunks and put into the bottom of the dish.

Fill up with the cold boiled chicken, cut into pieces.

Season with salt and pepper.

Roll out the pastry for the lid.

Moisten the edges and seal.

Make a hole in the centre for the steam to escape.

Brush with beaten egg to glaze.

Bake in a moderately hot oven for 1½ hours.

After baking brush again with beaten egg.

Bring 1 pint (600 ml/ 2½ cups) strained chicken stock to the boil and mix with the gelatine.

Pour through the hole in the lid.

Leave the pie to cool and serve cold.

Oven: 400°F/200°C Gas Mark 6

YOUNG CHICKENS IN A BLANKET Serves 8

This Worcestershire recipe from the 18th century is the same as a French blanquette — hence its name.

2 young chicken
1 lemon
A pinch of nutmeg
Salt and pepper
2 oz (50 g) butter
2 oz (50 g) flour
Cayenne pepper
2 tablespoons double cream
Sippets of fried bread

Truss the chickens and put them into enough hot water to cover them.

Simmer until half cooked.

Lift out, untruss and cut into quarters.

Add the peel and juice of the lemon to the broth.

Season with nutmeg, salt and pepper.

Return the chicken pieces to the broth and simmer until cooked.

Lift out on to a serving dish and keep warm.

Strain the broth and measure out 1 pint (600 ml/ 2½ cups).

Melt the butter in a saucepan and stir in the flour.

Cook gently for 2 minutes, but do not let it brown.

Remove from the heat and stir in the strained broth.

Return to the heat and bring to the boil, stirring all the time to avoid lumps.

Season with cayenne pepper and salt.

Add the cream.

Pour the broth over the chicken pieces.

Serve with sippets of fried bread.

To make fried sippets:

Cut stale bread into cubes.

Put the bread cubes into a frying basket.

Fry in hot oil until golden brown.

EVESHAM CHICKEN

Serves 4

4 chicken pieces
1 oz (25 g) seasoned flour
2 oz (50 g) butter
1 onion, peeled and chopped
2 red-skinned eating apples, cored and sliced
¾ pint (450 ml/ 2 cups) dry cider
2 teaspoons mixed herbs
Salt and pepper
¼ pint (150 ml/ ⅔ cup) single cream
1 tablespoon chopped parsley

Toss the chicken pieces in the seasoned flour.

Melt the butter in a frying pan and fry the chicken pieces on all sides.

Remove to a casserole dish.

Fry the onion and apples and add to the casserole.

Add any remaining flour to the fat in the frying pan and cook gently for 2-3 minutes.

Gradually stir in the cider, so that the sauce is free from lumps.

Add the herbs and season to taste with salt and pepper.

Remove from the heat and stir in the cream.

Pour the sauce over the chicken and vegetables in the casserole dish.

Cover and cook in a moderately hot oven for 1¼ hours.

Garnish with chopped parsley before serving.

Oven: 375°F/190°C Gas Mark 5

HEREFORD PIGEON PIE

Serves 4

2 medium or 3 small pigeons
12 oz (350 g) stewing beef
2 carrots
2 onions
Salt and pepper
6 oz (175 g) shortcrust pastry

Pluck, clean and joint the pigeons.

Cut the beef into small cubes.

Dice the onions and carrots.

Put all the ingredients into a large saucepan and cover with water.

Season well with salt and pepper.

Bring to the boil and simmer for 2½ hours, or until tender.

Remove the meat and vegetables from the liquid and put into a 1½ pint (900 ml) pie dish.

Add a couple of tablespoons of stock to moisten.

Roll out the pastry to make a lid.

Bake in a moderately hot oven for about 40 minutes, or until nicely browned.

Oven: 375°F/190°C Gas Mark 5

JUGGED PIGEONS

Serves 4

An 18th century recipe from Worcester.

4 pigeons
1 pint (600 ml/ 2½ cups) water
1 glass of beer
A bunch of fresh herbs
1 onion
1 oz (25 g) butter
1 oz (25 g) flour

For the stuffing:
4 oz (100 g) fresh white breadcrumbs
1 oz (25 g) shredded suet
4 hard-boiled egg yolks
1 dessertspoon chopped herbs — sweet marjoram, sage
  or rosemary
A little grated lemon peel
A pinch of nutmeg
Salt and pepper

Pluck and draw the birds.

Boil the livers and chop them finely.

Make the stuffing using the chopped livers, breadcrumbs,
suet, egg yolks, herbs, lemon peel and nutmeg.

Season with salt and pepper.

Divide the stuffing between the birds.

Put the stuffed birds into a large casserole dish and cover
with the water and beer.

Add the fresh herbs and peeled onion.

Put into a moderate oven for about 2 hours, or until the
pigeons are tender.

Remove from the oven and strain off the gravy.

Melt the butter in a saucepan.

Stir in the flour and cook gently for 2 minutes.

Gradually stir in 1 pint (600 ml) of the gravy.

Bring to the boil, stirring all the time, until the gravy thickens.

Pour over the pigeons.

Serve garnished with pickles.

Oven: 350°F/180°C Gas Mark 4

RABBIT STEW WITH FORCEMEAT
FORCEMEAT BALLS
Serves 6-8

This traditional dish is cooked in local cider. A little cider brandy may also be added to give it extra punch.

1 young rabbit
1 oz (25 g) seasoned flour
2 oz (50 g) butter
3 onions, thinly sliced
2 tablespoons chopped fresh herbs — a mixture of thyme, basil and marjoram
1 tablespoon chopped parsley
½ pint (300 ml/ 1¼ cups) cider
Salt and pepper

For the forcemeat balls:
Heart and liver of the rabbit
4 oz (100 g) streaky bacon
4 oz (100 g) fresh white breadcrumbs
2 oz (50 g) shredded suet
1 tablespoon chopped fresh herbs
1 tablespoon chopped parsley
Grated rind of 1 lemon
Salt and pepper
1 egg, beaten

Cut the rabbit into joints, reserving the heart and liver for the forcemeat balls.

Roll the joints in seasoned flour.

Melt the butter in a large frying pan and cook the chopped onion until soft.

Add the rabbit joints and brown on all sides.

Add the chopped herbs and parsley, and cider.

Season with salt and pepper.

Transfer to a casserole and cook in a cool oven for 2 hours, or until tender.

Meanwhile mince together the heart and liver of the rabbit and the streaky bacon.

Mix with the breadcrumbs, suet, chopped herbs, parsley and grated lemon rind.

Season with salt and pepper.

Bind together with the beaten egg.

Make the forcemeat into small balls and sauté gently in some melted butter.

Add the balls to the casserole 5 minutes before taking it out of the oven.

Check the seasoning before serving.

Oven: 275°F/140°C Gas Mark 1

HARVEST PUDDING

Serves 6-8

Rabbits were easy victims for the farmworkers when the corn was cut. This filling pudding was often made at harvest time.

1 large or 2 small rabbits
1 lb (450 g) self-raising flour
Salt and pepper
6 oz (175 g) butter, straight from the fridge
4 oz (50 g) suet
2 eggs, beaten with a little water
4 oz (100 g) chopped onions
8 oz (225 g) sliced mushrooms
8 oz (225 g) diced bacon
A pinch of sage
¼ pint (150 ml/ ⅔ cup) stock

Grease a 3½-4 pint (2-2.25 litre) pudding basin.

Cut the rabbit into joints.

Sieve the flour into a mixing basin.

Add a pinch of salt and pepper.

Grate the cold butter and stir into the flour with the suet.

Make a well in the centre and pour in the egg and water mixture.

Bring the flour in from the sides until it forms a soft dough.

Turn out on to a well-floured work surface.

Roll out three-quarters of the dough to line the pudding basin.

Fill with layers of rabbit joints, chopped onions, sliced mushrooms and diced bacon, seasoning each layer with salt, pepper and sage.

Pour over the stock.

Roll out the remaining pastry to make a lid.

Seal the edges firmly.

Cover with greaseproof paper and a pudding cloth.

Place in a pan with a small amount of boiling water and steam for 2 hours.

Add more boiling water if required, but do not allow the water to boil over the top of the pudding.

Turn the pudding out on to a dish to serve.

ROAST HARE

This is an early 18th century recipe from Worcester.

'Let him be well cleaned with the pudding thus:
Sweet herbs, bacon, lemon peel, two anchovies and the liver (if sound) par-boiled all chopt fine, beef suet, bread-crumbs seasoned with what spice you please, mixt all together with butter and put into the belly, truss and roast him, basting him, with a quart of rough cider or milk. Put good gravy under him in the dish.'

SPICED BEEF

The white-faced Hereford cattle are a cross between the native red long-horned cattle and cattle brought in from the Low Countries in the 17th century. This dish was once made all over England, and is still made in the prime beef-producing areas of the country, particularly at Christmas time.

A piece of silverside weighing 5-6 lbs (2.25-2.75 kg)
3 oz (75 g) soft dark brown sugar
1 heaped teaspoon saltpetre
4 oz (100 g) sea salt
1 oz (25 g) black peppercorns
1 oz (25 g) allspice
1 oz (25 g) juniper berries
½ pint (300 ml/ 1¼ cups) water
4 oz (100 g) shredded suet

Rub the beef all over with the brown sugar and put it into a close-fitting casserole dish.

Leave for two days in the refrigerator, turning it twice a day.

Crush the other ingredients together and rub into the beef on the third day.

Leave to marinate for a further nine days, turning regularly.

Before cooking the beef wipe off any bits that are clinging to it, but do not wash.

Put it back into the casserole dish with ½ pint (300 ml/ 1¼ cups) water.

Cover the top of the beef with the suet to keep it moist during cooking.

Put two layers of foil over the top.

Put the lid on tightly.

Bake in a cool oven for 4½ hours.

Remove from the oven and leave to cool for 3 hours without taking off the lid.

Then remove the lid and foil, drain the beef and wipe with kitchen paper.

Wrap loosely in clean foil and put a weight on top. Leave for at least 24 hours.

Wrap the spiced beef in greaseproof paper and store in the refrigerator until required — it will keep for up to three weeks.

Slice thinly to serve.

Oven: 275°F/140°C Gas Mark 4

SHIN OF BEEF STEW WITH DUMPLINGS

Serves 6-8

2 lb (900 g) shin of beef
1 oz (25 g) lard
1 oz (25 g) flour
2 pints (1.15 litres) beef stock
1 large onion, peeled and sliced
8 oz (225 g) carrots
Salt and pepper

For the dumplings:
4 oz (100 g) plain flour
1 teaspoon baking powder
A pinch of salt
2 oz (50 g) shredded suet
1 tablespoon chopped parsley
Cold water

Cut the meat into ¾ inch (2 cm) cubes.

Melt the lard in a large saucepan.

When hot, fry the cubes of meat quickly on all sides.

Sprinkle over the flour and stir.

Cook gently for 2 minutes.

Stir in the beef stock and bring to the boil.

Add the sliced onion and chopped carrots.

Season well with salt and pepper.

Cover and simmer for about 2 hours, or until the meat is tender.

To make the dumplings:

Sift the flour, baking powder and salt together.

Mix in the suet, chopped parsley, and enough water to make a soft dough.

With floured hands roll the dough into 8 little balls.

Add the dumplings to the stew for the last 20 minutes of cooking time.

POTTED BEEF

This is an early 18th century recipe from Worcester.

Bake a tender piece of beef in butter till very tender. Drain it from the gravy, season it with cloves, mace, nutmeg, pepper and salt. Pound it in a stone mortar with a wooden beater adding fresh butter; when smooth and fine put it in your pots, close, clear the oyl'd butter from the gravy and pour over; if not enough oyle melt some butter and pour over.

BEEF OLIVES

Serves 4

An old 18th century recipe from Worcester reads: 'Cutt some square steakes of beef, wash them with some egg, season them lay on forcemeat. Role them up and tie them and either roast or stew them. Pour over them some good gravy with shallots, chopt fine in it. Garnish with pickles.'

This is a more modern version.

1 lb (450 g) rump steak
3 oz (75 g) fresh white breadcrumbs
1 oz (25 g) shredded suet
1 tablespoon chopped parsley
2 anchovies, chopped
1 teaspoon lemon juice
1 egg
Salt and pepper
1 oz (25 g) lard
1 oz (25 g) flour
1 pint (600 ml/ 2½ cups) beef stock

Cut the meat into four slices and flatten them with a rolling pin.

Mix together the breadcrumbs, suet, parsley, anchovies, lemon juice and egg to make a forcemeat stuffing.

Season well with salt and pepper.

Divide the stuffing into four and spread on each slice of steak.

Roll up tightly and tie with fine string or thread.

Melt the lard in a frying pan and fry the meat rolls until brown on all sides.

Remove from the pan and drain.

Stir the flour into the remaining fat in the pan and cook gently for 2 minutes.

Gradually stir in the hot stock, taking care to avoid lumps.

Bring to the boil.

Season with salt and pepper.

Add the meat rolls and simmer for 1 hour.

When cooked, remove the string from the meat.

Serve with the gravy on a bed of mashed potatoes.

BRAISED BEEF IN ONION SAUCE

Serves 6

3 lb (1.5 kg) rolled topside or brisket of beef
2 cloves of garlic
¼ pint (150 ml/ ⅔ cup) oil
2 oz (50 g) butter
1 small onion, finely chopped
4 young turnips, peeled and chopped
1 bay leaf
1½ pints (900 ml/ 3¾ cups) stock

For the marinade:
Juice and rind of ½ lemon
1 onion, sliced
2 level teaspoons brown sugar
1 teaspoon chopped fresh mixed herbs
1 level teaspoon salt
A pinch of cayenne pepper

For the sauce:
8 onions, sliced
2 oz (50 g) butter
1 level teaspoon salt
½ level teaspoon grated nutmeg
2 tablespoons mashed potato
2 oz (50 g) plain flour
1 pint (600 ml/ 2½ cups) milk
Watercress to garnish

Rub the meat with the crushed garlic.

Mix together the marinade ingredients.

Pour over the meat and leave for 3 or 4 hours, turning from time to time.

Remove from the marinade and pat dry.

Melt the butter in a large saucepan.

Add the chopped onion and the garlic and fry gently for a few minutes.

Add the turnips, bay leaf and stock.

Put in the beef, bring to the boil and simmer gently for 2½ hours, or until tender.

Drain the meat and keep hot.

To make the sauce melt the butter in a saucepan and add the sliced onions.

Season with salt, pepper and nutmeg.

Cook gently for 20 minutes, or until the onions are soft but not browned.

Add the mashed potato, flour and milk.

Stir thoroughly to make a sauce.

Pour the sauce round the meat.

Garnish with the watercress before serving.

GALANTINE

1 lb (450 g) stewing steak
8 oz (225 g) collar of bacon
2 oz (50 g) breadcrumbs
1 beaten egg
3 tablespoons milk
Salt and pepper

For the dressing:
2 tablespoons vinegar
2 teaspoons sugar
1 small onion
1 small lettuce

Grease a 1½ pint (900 ml) pudding basin.

Mince the steak and the bacon.

Add the breadcrumbs.

Mix in the beaten egg and the milk.

Season well with salt and pepper.

Spoon the mixture into the greased pudding basin.

Cover with greaseproof paper.

Steam for 3 hours.

Remove the greaseproof paper and put a saucer with a heavy weight on it on top of the meat.

Leave until quite cold.

To make the dressing:

Put the sugar into a small basin and pour over the vinegar.

Stir until the sugar has dissolved.

Chop the onion and lettuce very finely and toss in the vinegar.

STEAK AND KIDNEY PUDDING   Serves 4

12 oz (350 g) stewing steak
4 oz (100 g) lambs' kidneys
1 oz (25 g) seasoned flour
1 onion
3 tablespoons water

For the pastry:
8 oz (225 g) self-raising flour
A pinch of salt
4 oz (100 g) shredded suet
Cold water

Grease a 1½ pint (900 ml) pudding basin.

Cut the stewing steak into ¾ inch (2 cm) cubes.

Core and slice the lambs' kidneys.

Toss both in the seasoned flour.

Peel and slice the onion.

To make the pastry, sift the flour and salt into a mixing basin.

Add the suet and enough cold water to make a soft dough.

Roll out two-thirds of the pastry to line the pudding basin.

Fill with the meat and onions.

Add the water.

Roll out the remaining pastry to make a lid.

Dampen the edges and seal them.

Cover with greased greaseproof paper.

Put into a large saucepan of boiling water and steam for about 4 hours.

Serve hot.

STEAK AND KIDNEY PIE

2 lb (900 g) chuck steak
8 oz (225 g) lambs' kidneys
1 oz (25 g) seasoned flour
2 oz (50 g) butter
1 lb (450 g) onions
½ pint (300 ml/ 1¼ cups) beef stock
2 tablespoons sherry
A bouquet garni
12 oz (350 g) shortcrust pastry
Beaten egg to glaze

Cut the steak into ¾ inch (2 cm) cubes.

Core and slice the kidneys.

Toss in the seasoned flour.

Melt the butter in a frying pan and brown the steak and kidneys quickly.

Remove from the pan to a casserole dish.

Peel and slice the onions and add to the frying pan.

Cook gently until softened.

Mix with the meat in the casserole dish.

Blend any remaining flour into the fat in the pan.

Stir in the stock and bring to the boil.

Pour over the meat in the casserole.

Add the sherry and bouquet garni.

Cover the dish and cook in a moderate oven for about 2 hours, or until the meat is tender.

Remove the meat from the casserole with a slotted spoon and transfer to a 2½ pint (1.5 litre) pie dish.

Boil the remaining meat juices until they are reduced to ½ pint (300 ml/ 1¼ cups).

Pour over the meat and allow to cool.

Roll out the pastry to cover the pie dish, supporting it with a pie funnel if the meat comes below the rim of the dish.

Use any trimmings to decorate the top.

Brush the top with beaten egg to glaze.

Bake in a hot oven for 30 minutes, then reduce the temperature and bake for a further hour.

The pie can be eaten hot or cold.

Oven: 325°F/160°C Gas Mark 3

Then: 425°F/220°C Gas Mark 7

Reduce to: 350°F/180°C Gas Mark 4

HEREFORD PIGGIES IN THE GRASS

Serves 6-8

In days gone by pigs were put to root about in the Herefordshire orchards, feeding on windfall apples. This is a local pork speciality.

2 or 3 pork fillets, weighing about 2 lb (900 g)
1 oz (25 g) flour, seasoned with garlic salt and pepper
3 oz (75 g) butter
1 onion, peeled and sliced
2 eating apples, peeled and sliced
¼ pint (150 ml/ ⅔ cup) dry cider
¼ pint (150 ml/ ⅔ cup) stock
3 tablespoons cream
Cooked asparagus spears to garnish

For the stuffing:
1 lambs' kidney, minced
2 oz (50 g) cooked ham, minced
1 clove garlic, crushed
4 oz (100 g) cooked spinach, chopped
1 egg, beaten
A pinch of allspice
Salt and black pepper

Split the pork fillets and beat them flat with a rolling pin.

Mix together the stuffing ingredients.

Spread the stuffing evenly over each fillet, roll up and secure.

All in the seasoned flour.

Melt the butter in a large frying pan and brown the fillets all over.

Remove from the pan and add the sliced onion and apples.

Fry gently for a few minutes.

Stir in the remaining flour.

Add the cider and stock.

Bring to the boil.

Add the pork fillets and simmer for 45 minutes, or until the meat is tender.

Add the cream, but do not allow to boil.

Check the seasoning.

Place on a serving dish and garnish with asparagus spears.

LOVE IN DISGUISE

Serves 6-8

This dish of baked stuffed calf hearts was popular in the 18th century. The coating of vermicelli and breadcrumbs hides the hearts.

4 calf hearts
8 oz (225 g) veal forcemeat
12 rashers fat bacon
4 oz (100 g) vermicelli
2 oz (50 g) fresh white breadcrumbs
1 egg
2 oz (50 g) lard

For the veal forcemeat:
8 oz (225 g) fillet of veal
4 oz (100 g) uncooked ham or gammon
4 oz (100 g) fresh white breadcrumbs
2 tablespoons finely chopped parsley
Salt and pepper
1 egg

Cut the flaps, gristle and tubes from the hearts, and snip out the membranes that divide the hearts inside.

Soak in cold water for 2 hours.

Wash, and then soak in fresh water for 30 minutes.

Meanwhile make the stuffing.

Mince the veal and chop the ham finely.

Mix with the breadcrumbs and parsley.

Season with salt and pepper.

Bind together with the lightly beaten egg.

Stuff the mixture into the cleaned calfs' hearts and sew up the openings with thread or fine string.

Wrap the bacon rashers around the hearts and secure with wooden skewers.

Wrap in aluminium foil and place in a roasting tin.

Bake in a moderate oven for 1½ hours.

Break the vermicelli into small pieces and boil until soft in salted water.

Drain, cool, and mix with the breadcrumbs.

Remove the hearts from the oven, cool slightly and brush with beaten egg.

Coat the hearts with the vermicelli and breadcrumb mixture.

Return the hearts, without foil, to the roasting tin.

Add the lard and bake for a further 30 minutes, or until the coating is crisp and brown.

Oven: 350°F/180°C Gas Mark 4

PIGS' FRY

When a pig was slaughtered the perishable offal parts — the liver, kidney, heart and brain — were used up immediately in this traditional dish.

1 lb (450 g) pigs' fry
1 oz (25 g) pork fat
2 onions
1 tablespoon chopped sage
Salt and pepper
1 oz (25 g) cornflour

Cut the fry into small pieces and place in an ovenproof dish.

Add the pork fat, sliced onions and chopped sage.

Season with salt and pepper.

Bake in a moderate oven for about 1 hour.

Strain off the cooking liquid into a saucepan.

Mix the cornflour with a little water and add to the cooking liquid.

Bring to the boil, stirring, until the gravy has thickened.

Pour over the pigs' fry and serve hot.

Oven: 350°F/180°C Gas Mark 4

BRAWN

1 pig's head
1 lb (450 g) leg of beef
1 onion
Salt and pepper
A pinch each of powdered cloves and mace

Clean the head well and soak in cold water for a couple of hours.

Drain off the water and place the pig's head in a large saucepan.

Add the beef cut into smallish pieces, and the chopped onion.

Cover with fresh water.

Season with salt, pepper, cloves and mace.

Bring to the boil and simmer until the meat falls away from the bone — about 3 hours.

Take out the head and remove all the meat quickly before it gets cold and sets.

Roughly chop the meat, including the beef, and put it into a wet mould.

Put the bones back into the cooking liquid and boil rapidly until it has reduced by half its volume.

Pour some of the hot liquid over the meat in the mould.

Leave to cool and set.

Turn out on to a serving dish.

(The rest of the cooking liquid makes excellent soup.)

ASPARAGUS

The Vale of Evesham is famous for its asparagus, which is in season from May to early July. The thin stems of Worcestershire asparagus are easily distinguishable from the fat green asparagus grown in Norfolk, Suffolk and Essex. Allow 8-12 stems per person.

To cook asparagus:

Trim the stems into equal lengths and scrape the white ends lightly, from the tip downwards.

Tie the stems into bundles with soft string.

Stand the bundles upright in sufficient boiling water to cover the stems, with the tips above water.

Add a little salt and a lump of sugar.

Cook for 5-8 minutes, or until tender.

Drain thoroughly and remove the string.

Serve hot with melted butter.

KIDNEY BEAN SALAD

1 lb (450 g) kidney beans
1 small slice streaky bacon
1 small onion, finely chopped
1 sprig of parsley, finely chopped
1 tablespoon cream or milk
1 teaspoon vinegar
Salt and pepper

Slice the beans and boil until cooked.

Drain and leave to cool.

Chop the bacon into small pieces and fry until lightly browned.

Added the finely chopped onion and parsley to the beans.

Stir in the milk and the vinegar.

Season with salt and pepper.

Mix in the fried bacon.

MARINADED BEETROOT

1 medium-sized cooked beetroot
3 tablespoons wine vinegar
1 tablespoon water
2 teaspoons caster sugar
1 clove of garlic, crushed
4 cloves

Cut the cooked beetroot into small cubes and put into a small serving bowl.

Dissolve the sugar in the vinegar and water.

Add the garlic and cloves and pour over the beetroot.

Leave overnight before serving.

CRAYFISH AND BACON SAVOURY   Serves 8

Crayfish were once plentiful in Herefordshire rivers and can still be found in some.

16 crayfish tails
1 lb (450 g) bacon rashers
Salt and pepper
8 slices toast

Remove the meat from the tails of the crayfish and cut into small pieces.

Dice the bacon and fry gently, without any extra fat, in a frying pan.

When the fat is running freely add the crayfish meat.

Cook for a few minutes to heat through.

Season with salt and pepper.

Pour over hot buttered toast.

ASPARAGUS AND EGGS

Serves 4

12 oz (350 g) asparagus tips
4 slices of bread
8 eggs
Salt and pepper

Cook the asparagus tips in boiling, salted water.

Drain and keep warm.

Toast the bread, butter it and lay it on a hot dish.

Beat the eggs and season with salt and pepper.

Scramble them with a tablespoon of butter, so that they are creamy.

Arrange three-quarters of the asparagus on the toast. Spoon the scrambled egg on top.

Decorate with the remaining asparagus.

EGG SAVOURY

Serves 2

The slices of bread for this tasty supper dish should be at least 1 inch (2.5 cm) thick.

2 thick slices of bread
2 eggs
Grated cheese

Toast one side of the slices of bread.

On the untoasted side, scoop out a hole and break an egg into it.

Cover the egg and bread with grated cheese.

Brown under a hot grill.

Serve piping hot.

SUPPER SAVOURY

Serves 2

2 thick slices of bread
2 slices of cheese
Mustard
A dash of Worcestershire sauce
Salt
2 tomatoes
2 slices of bacon

Put the slices of cheese on the bread.

Spread with a little mustard.

Sprinkle over the Worcestershire sauce and a little salt.

Slice the tomatoes and arrange on top of the bread.

Lay a slice of bacon on top of each slice.

Place on a hot baking tray and bake in a hot oven for about 15 minutes, or until the bacon is crisp.

Oven: 400°F/200°C Gas Mark 6

SPICED PEARS IN CIDER

Serves 8

8 Conference pears
Lemon juice
8 oz (225 g) granulated sugar
4 tablespoons water
A stick of cinnamon
¼ pint (150 ml/ ⅔ cup) dry Hereford cider
2 cloves
A strip of orange rind

Peel the pears, leaving them whole and the stems intact.

Sprinkle with lemon juice to prevent them discolouring.

Put the sugar, water and cinnamon stick into a saucepan and heat slowly until the sugar dissolves.

Bring to the boil.

Add the peeled pears, cider, cloves and orange rind.

Bring back to the boil, cover, and simmer very gently until the pears are tender but not overcooked.

Transfer the pears to a serving dish.

Continue boiling the liquid until it has reduced to a thick syrup.

Strain the syrup over the pears.

Chill, and serve with cream.

PLUM CHARLOTTE

Serves 4

1 lb (450 g) plums
1 small sliced loaf of bread
2 oz (50 g) butter
4 oz (100 g) brown sugar

Wash, halve and stone the plums.

Grease a shallow 1 pint (500 ml) pie dish.

Butter the slices of bread and use some of them to line the base and sides of the dish.

Sprinkle over some of the sugar.

Cover with halved plums, cut side uppermost.

Sprinkle over more sugar and add more plums until they are all used up.

Cover with the remaining slices of buttered bread.

Bake in a moderate oven for 20-30 minutes.

Serve hot or cold with cream.

Oven: 350°F/180°C Gas Mark 4

PLUM CRUMBLE

Serves 4-6

1 lb (450 g) plums
2 oz (225 g) sugar
6 oz (175 g) self-raising flour
3 oz (75 g) butter or margarine
3 oz (75 g) demerara sugar

Halve the plums and remove the stones.

Put into a saucepan with a little water and the sugar and simmer gently until soft.

Sift the flour into a mixing basin.

Rub in the butter or margarine so that the mixture looks like coarse breadcrumbs.

Stir in the demerara sugar.

Put the stewed plums and 4 tablespoons of the juice into a pie dish.

Spread over the crumble topping.

Bake in a moderately hot oven for 35-40 minutes.

Serve hot or cold, with custard or cream.

Oven: 375°F/190°C Gas Mark 5

MALVERN APPLE PUDDING

Serves 6-8

4 oz (100 g) sugar
4 oz (100 g) butter
2 beaten eggs
4 oz (100 g) flour
A pinch of salt
8 oz (225 g) russet apples
Grated rind of 1 lemon
1 oz (40 g) currants
2 tablespoons brandy

Grease a 2½-3 pint (1.5 litre) pudding basin.

Beat the sugar and butter together until light and fluffy.

Beat in the eggs, adding a little of the flour to stop curdling.

Fold in the sifted flour and salt.

Peel, core and finely chop the apples.

Fold into the mixture with the lemon rind, currants and brandy.

Spoon into the pudding basin.

Cover with greaseproof paper.

Steam for 1½ hours.

Turn out and serve warm with custard.

MALVERN PUDDING

Serves 6-8

3 oz (75 g) butter
1½ oz (40 g) flour
1 pint (600 ml/ 2½ cups) warm milk
1 lb (450 g) stewed apples
2 oz (50 g) caster sugar
A pinch of ground cinnamon

Grease a 2½ pint (1.5 litre) pie dish.

Melt half the butter in a saucepan.

Stir in the flour.

Gradually add the milk, stirring all the time until thick and smooth.

Put layers of stewed apple and pudding mixture alternately in the greased pie dish, finishing with a layer of pudding.

Dot the top with the remaining butter.

Sprinkle over the sugar and the cinnamon.

Bake in a moderate oven for 20 minutes.

Place under a hot grill to brown the top before serving.

Oven: 350°F/180°C Gas Mark 4

BAKED APPLE PUDDING

Serves 6-8

8 oz (225 g) peeled, cored and sliced apples
4 oz (100 g) sugar
Grated rind and juice of 1 lemon
8 oz (225 g) creamed butter
2 eggs
2 egg yolks
8 oz (225 g) shortcrust pastry
Candied lemon and orange peel

Put the prepared apples and sugar into a saucepan and simmer gently until reduced to a pulp.

Add the lemon juice and rind.

Stir in the creamed butter.

Beat the eggs together with the two egg yolks.

Stir into the apple mixture.

Roll out the pastry to line an 8 inch (20 cm) flan ring.

Fill with the apple mixture.

Decorate the top with candied peel.

Bake in a moderately hot oven for about 40 minutes, or until set and firm.

Oven: 375°F/190°C Gas Mark 5

WHORTLEBERRY AND CROWBERRY PUDDING

Serves 6

Whortleberries and crowberries are plentiful in Herefordshire.

1-1½ lb (450-675 g) whortleberries and crowberries
2-3 oz (50-75 g) sugar
8 oz (225 g) plain flour
1 teaspoon baking powder
A pinch of salt
3 oz (75 g) shredded suet

Prepare the fruit and mix it with the sugar.

Sift the flour with the baking powder and salt into a mixing basin.

Add the suet.

Mix with sufficient water to make a soft, but firm dough.

Roll out to make a lid.

Grease and line a pudding basin.

Fill to the top with the fruit and sugar.

Add 2 tablespoons of water.

Put on the suet crust lid.

Cover with greaseproof paper and steam for 2½-3 hours.

WHITE LADIES PUDDING

Serves 6-8

This is a traditional Worcestershire pudding.

4 oz (100 g) desiccated coconut
6 thin slices of white bread, thickly buttered
1 pint (600 ml/ 2½ cups) milk
A few drops of vanilla essence
A pinch of salt
3 eggs
3 oz (75 g) sugar

Butter a 2½ pint (1.4 litre) pie dish.

Sprinkle with the desiccated coconut.

Remove the crusts from the bread and cut into triangles or squares.

Arrange in the pie dish.

Heat the milk and add the vanilla essence and salt.

Beat the eggs with the sugar.

Pour the heated milk over the beaten eggs and stir.

Pour over the bread in the pie dish.

Leave to soak for 30 minutes.

Place the pie dish in a tray of hot water.

Bake in a moderate oven for 30-40 minutes, or until set.

Oven: 350°F/180°C Gas Mark 4

BEASTINGS PUDDING

Serves 4

Beastings is the very rich milk, colostrum, given by a cow shortly after calving. A baked custard used to be made of this, without using any eggs. There was a curious bit of folklore connected with beastings. It could not be bought; the farmer's wife used to send a jugful to some of her oldest or best customers, and tell them not to wash out the jug. To return the jug washed was thought to bring about the death of the newborn calf. Here is a modern adaptation of the old recipe.

1 pint (600 ml/ 2½ cups) milk
1 tablespoon lemon juice (or rennet)
2 eggs
1 oz (25 g) caster sugar
1 cup of milk
Grated nutmeg

Heat the pint of milk almost to boiling point and add the lemon juice or rennet.

Leave overnight in a warm place for the milk to curdle.

Next day, strain off the whey through a muslin bag, leaving behind the curds.

Beat the eggs with the sugar.

Stir in the curds and the cup of milk.

Strain into an ovenproof dish.

Sprinkle with nutmeg.

Stand the dish in a tray of warm water.

Bake in a moderate oven for about 1 hour, or until the pudding is set.

Oven: 325°F/160°C Gas Mark 3

GRAN'S PARADISE PUDDING

Serves 4

Serve a sweet sauce with this delicious pudding.

3 cooking apples
4 oz (100 g) fresh white breadcrumbs
3 oz (75 g) sugar
3 oz (75 g) currants
Grated rind of half a lemon
A pinch of grated nutmeg
A pinch of salt
3 beaten eggs
½ wineglass of brandy

For the sauce:
1 teaspoon cornflour or arrowroot
½ pint (300ml/ 1¼ cups) milk
A strip of lemon rind
1 dessertspoon sugar

Butter a pudding basin.

Peel, core, and chop the apples into small pieces.

Mix with the breadcrumbs, sugar, currants, grated lemon rind, nutmeg and salt.

Pour over the beaten eggs and brandy and stir well.

Spoon the mixture into the buttered pudding basin.

Cover with greaseproof paper and a cloth.

Steam for 1½ hours.

To make the sauce:

Mix the cornflour or arrowroot with some of the milk.

Heat the remaining milk with the lemon rind.

Stir the heated milk into the cornflour mixture.

Return to the saucepan, bring to the boil and simmer for 5 minutes.

Remove the lemon rind.

Add the sugar.

Serve the sweet white sauce with the pudding.

APPLE DUMPLINGS

Serves 3

These traditional Worcestershire apple dumplings can be filled with raisins, brown sugar, golden syrup or mincemeat, but the apple stays nice and fluffy if cooked without sugar.

8 oz (225 g) self-raising flour
4 oz (100 g) suet
½ teaspoon baking powder
A pinch of salt
Cold water
3 medium-sized cooking apples

Mix together the flour, suet, baking powder and salt with enough cold water to make a soft dough.

Divide into three and roll out until large enough to enclose an apple.

Peel and core the apples.

Enclose each apple in pastry, sealing the edges with a little water.

Place the apple dumplings in a floured cloth and tie securely.

Put into a saucepan of boiling water and boil for 1½ hours.

Before serving slice through and sprinkle liberally with sugar.

Eat while hot.

FIG PUDDING WITH WINE SAUCE Serves 4

8 oz (225 g) figs
8 oz (225 g) fresh white breadcrumbs
8 oz (225 g) sugar
6 oz (175 g) suet
½ teaspoon grated nutmeg
2 beaten eggs

For the wine sauce:
Rind of half a lemon
1½ oz (40 g) sugar
1 wineglass water
1 oz (25 g) butter
1 teaspoon flour
1½ wineglasses sherry or Madeira

Grease a pudding basin.

Mince the figs very small.

Mix with the breadcrumbs, sugar, suet and nutmeg.

Stir in the well-beaten eggs.

Spoon into the greased pudding basin.

Cover with greaseproof paper.

Steam for 4½ hours.

To make the sauce:

Put the lemon peel, sugar and water into a saucepan.

Bring to the boil and simmer gently for 15 minutes.

Take out the lemon peel.

Knead the flour into the butter and stir into the sauce.

Add the sherry or Madeira.

Reheat, and serve immediately.

WORCESTERSHIRE PEAR SOUFFLÉ

Serves 8

One of the ingredients in this recipe is vanilla sugar. The easiest way of making this is to put four vanilla pods in a 2 lb (900 g) bottling jar and keep it filled up with caster sugar.

2 macaroons
1 large ripe pear
Juice of half a lemon
1 tablespoon kirsch or William pear brandy
4 oz (100 g) butter
4 oz (100 g) vanilla sugar
1 oz (25 g) cornflour
4 eggs

Grease a 2½ pint (1.5 litre) soufflé dish with buttered paper.

Crush the macaroons and shake half of the crumbs around the dish, reserving the other half for the top of the soufflé.

Peel, core and chop the pear to a juicy mash.

Mix in the lemon and the kirsch or pear brandy.

Put the butter in a basin, set it over a saucepan of simmering water and stir until it's melted.

Sieve the sugar and flour together.

Stir into the melted butter.

Separate the eggs.

Remove the basin from the heat and whisk in the egg yolks.

Then add the chopped pear and its juices.

Beat the egg whites until they are stiff.

Mix a tablespoon of the egg white vigorously into the pear mixture, then fold in the rest with a metal spoon.

Turn the mixture into the buttered soufflé dish.

Sprinkle the top with the remaining macaroon crumbs.

Bake in a hot oven for 3 minutes, then reduce the heat and bake for a further 27 minutes.

Do not open the oven door before at least 20 minutes has passed or the soufflé will fall.

GINGER MOULD

½ oz (15 g) gelatine
2 tablespoons hot water
½ pint (300 ml/ 1¼ cups) milk
2 oz (50 g) caster sugar
3 oz (75 g) butter
2 eggs
½ teaspoon ground ginger
Juice of 1 lemon
Preserved ginger and syrup

Dissolve the gelatine in the hot water.

Add it to the milk, sugar and butter.

Separate the eggs and beat the yolks.

Add the yolks to the mixture.

Put the mixture into a double saucepan and stir until thick, but do not allow to boil.

Add the ground ginger.

When nearly set, fold in the stiffly beaten egg whites and the lemon juice.

Pour the mixture into a wetted mould.

Leave to set.

When set turn out and serve with preserved ginger and syrup.

HEREFORD BRANDY SNAPS   Makes 18-20

Brandy snaps used to be known as 'jumbles', and even earlier as 'gaufres' or wafers. They were traditionally sold at fairs. This recipe was used for the brandy snaps sold at the Hereford Annual May Fair.

3 oz (75 g) butter
4 oz (100 g) sugar
4 oz (100 g) black treacle
4 oz (100 g) plain flour
½ teaspoon ground ginger
1 teaspoon brandy
A squeeze of lemon juice

Grease two baking sheets.

Put the butter, sugar and treacle into a saucepan and heat until melted.

Leave to cool.

Stir in the flour, ginger, brandy and lemon juice.

Mix very thoroughly.

Drop teaspoonsful of the mixture on to the greased baking sheets.

Bake in a moderate oven for 10 minutes until golden brown.

Remove from the oven, allow to cool slightly, and then lift off with a palette knife.

Roll each one quickly round the handle of a wooden spoon.

Lift off when set.

Oven: 350°F/180°C Gas Mark 4

HEREFORD CIDER CAKE

4 oz (100 g) butter
4 oz (100 g) caster sugar
2 eggs
8 oz (225 g) plain flour
½ teaspoon grated nutmeg
½ teaspoon bicarbonate of soda
¼ pint (150 ml/ ⅔ cup) cider

Grease and line an 8 inch (20 cm) cake tin.

Beat the butter and sugar until light and fluffy.

Stir in the eggs, one at a time, whisking well after each addition.

Sift the flour with the nutmeg and bicarbonate of soda and fold into the mixture.

Add the cider and mix well.

Turn into the cake tin and level the top.

Bake in a moderately hot oven for 1 hour.

Oven: 375°F/190°C Gas Mark 5

POUND CAKE

This makes a large, very rich fruit cake.

1 lb (450 g) flour
1 teaspoon baking powder
1 teaspoon mixed spice
½ teaspoon grated nutmeg
1 lb (450 g) butter
1 lb (450 g) sugar
8 eggs
1 lb (450 g) raisins
1 lb (450 g) sultanas
1 lb (450 g) currants
6 oz (175 g) cut mixed peel
2 tablespoons ground almonds
Grated rind of 1 lemon
1 glass of brandy

Grease and line a large cake tin.

Sift the flour, baking powder, mixed spice and nutmeg into a mixing basin.

Cream the butter and sugar together.

Add the eggs, one at a time, and a spoonful of flour with each addition to stop curdling.

Stir in the rest of the flour.

Add the fruit, almonds, lemon rind and brandy.

Spoon into the cake tin.

Bake in a moderate oven for about 4 hours — test by sticking a skewer into the centre.

Oven: 325°F/160°C Gas Mark 3

MELTING MOMENTS

4 oz (100 g) butter or margarine
1 oz (25 g) icing sugar
2 oz (50 g) self-raising flour
2 oz (50 g) cornflour
A few drops of vanilla essence
Butter icing

Grease 2 baking trays.

Beat the butter and sugar together.

Add the flours and the vanilla essence.

Put the mixture into a forcing bag and make about 20 rosettes on the baking trays.

Bake in a moderate oven for 10-12 minutes, until very pale brown in colour.

Leave on the trays to cool.

Sandwich pairs together with a little butter icing.

Oven: 350°F/180°C Gas Mark 4

HEREFORD CURD CAKE

This is a good way of using up milk that has gone sour — milk can be soured by adding a tablespoon of lemon juice or rennet.

1 pint (600 ml/ 2½ cups) milk
1 tablespoon lemon juice or rennet
6 oz (175 g) shortcrust pastry
1 oz (25 g) butter
1 egg, beaten
1 dessertspoon brandy or rum
1 teaspoon grated lemon rind
1 oz (25 g) currants
½ oz (15 g) caster sugar
A pinch of grated nutmeg

If using fresh milk, heat it almost to boiling point and add the lemon juice or rennet.

Leave overnight in a warm place for the milk to curdle.

Strain off the whey through a muslin bag, leaving behind the curds.

Roll out the pastry to line a sandwich tin.

Beat the curds and the butter together.

Add the beaten egg, brandy, lemon rind, currants and caster sugar.

Spoon the mixture into the pastry case.

Sprinkle with grated nutmeg.

Bake in a moderately hot oven for 10 minutes, then reduce the heat and bake for another 30 minutes, or until the mixture is set and the pastry is cooked.

Oven: 400°F/200°C Gas Mark 6

Reduce to: 350°F/180°C Gas Mark 4

SEED CAKE

Caraway seeds are often used as flavouring in traditional Herefordshire baking.

8 oz (225 g) self-raising flour
6 oz (175 g) caster sugar
6 oz (175 g) butter
3 eggs
2 teaspoons caraway seeds
1 heaped tablespoon ground almonds
A little milk
4 oz (100 g) candied lemon peel

Grease and line a medium-sized loaf tin.

Sift the flour into a mixing basin.

Cream the sugar and butter together until pale and creamy.

Add the eggs one at a time, with a spoonful of flour.

Add the caraway seeds and ground almonds.

Fold in the rest of the flour and add enough milk to keep the mixture soft.

Spoon the mixture into the tin and level it off with a knife.

Decorate the top with candied lemon peel.

Bake in the centre of a moderate oven for about 1 hour, or until the cake is springy to the touch.

Allow to cool in the tin before turning out on to a wire rack.

Oven: 350°F/180°C Gas Mark 4

GINGERBREAD

4 oz (100 g) butter
2 oz (50 g) brown sugar
8 oz (225 g) black treacle
2 eggs
10 oz (275 g) self-raising flour
A pinch of ground cloves
A pinch of ground mace
1 teaspoon ground ginger
1 teaspoon caraway seeds
1 tablespoon mixed peel
2 tablespoons raisins

Grease and line a medium-sized cake tin.

Melt the butter and mix with the sugar and treacle.

Add the eggs one at a time.

Sift the flour with the ground cloves, mace and ginger.

Fold into the treacle mixture.

Add the caraway seeds, mixed peel and raisins.

Spoon the mixture into the cake tin.

Bake in a moderate oven for 1½ hours.

Oven: 325°F/160°C Gas Mark 3

ALMOND CAKE

3 oz (75 g) butter
3 oz (75 g) margarine
3 oz (75 g) self-raising flour
3 oz (75 g) ground almonds
6 oz (175 g) sugar
3 beaten eggs

Soften the butter and margarine.

Stir in the flour and ground almonds.

Add the sugar.

Beat in the eggs.

Spoon the mixture into a greased and lined cake tin.

Bake in a moderate oven for 1-1¼ hours, until firm to the touch.

Oven: 350°F/180°C Gas Mark 4

QUINCE MARMALET

This is a Worcester cook's recipe from the early 18th century.

Approx 1 lb (450 g) quinces
Approx 1 lb (450 g) loaf sugar
Approx 1 pint (600 ml/ 2½ cups) water

Peel the quinces, cut into quarters and core them.

Leave in cold water so that they do not discolour.

Put the peel and cores into a saucepan and cover with cold water.

Bring to the boil and simmer until tender.

Strain off the liquid.

Leave to cool.

Measure the liquid and weigh the peeled quinces.

For every 1 pint (600 ml/ 2½ cups) water you need 1 lb (450 g) fruit and l lb (450 g) sugar.

Put all the ingredients into a saucepan, bring to the boil, cover, and simmer until tender.

Pour into warmed jars.

When cold cover with greaseproof paper soaked in a little brandy.

GOOOSEBERRY RELISH

2 lb (900 g) gooseberries
1 lb (450 g) onions
12 oz (350 g) seedless raisins
8 oz (225 g) brown sugar
1 teaspoon dry mustard
1 tablespoon ground ginger
2 tablespoons salt
¼ teaspoon Cayenne pepper
2 teaspoons turmeric
1 pint (600 ml/ 2½ cups) brown malt vinegar

Top and tail the gooseberries.

Mince the gooseberries with the onions and raisins.

Put into a saucepan with the sugar, mustard, ginger, salt, Cayenne pepper, turmeric and vinegar.

Bring slowly to the boil.

Simmer for 45 minutes.

Put the mixture through a coarse sieve.

Reheat thoroughly.

Pour into bottles and cork.

Use as required.

SWEET-SOUR PLUM SAUCE

4 lbs (1.75 kg) Pershore plums
8 oz (225 g) onions
1 pint (600 ml/ 2½ cups) brown malt vinegar
1 oz (25 g) salt
½ oz (15 g) each ground ginger, allspice, nutmeg and
    dry mustard powder
8 oz (225 g) sugar

Stone and cut up the plums.

Peel and chop the onions.

Put into a saucepan with the vinegar, salt and spices.

Bring to the boil and simmer for 30 minutes.

Sieve, stir in the sugar, and bring back to the boil.

Simmer for a further hour, stirring occasionally.

Bottle while still warm.

Use as required.

ASPARAGUS SAUCE

This delicate, creamy sauce goes well with poultry and fish dishes.

1 lb (675 g) asparagus
2 oz (50 g) butter
Juice of half a lemon
¼ pint (150 ml/ ⅔ cup) double cream
2 egg yolks
Salt and pepper

For the white sauce:
3 oz (75 g) butter or margarine
3 oz (75 g) flour
1 pint (600 ml/ 2½ cups) milk
1 pint (600 ml/ 2½ cups) chicken stock

Clean the asparagus and cook gently in the butter for 3-4 minutes.

Cut into pieces, reserving some of the tips for garnish.

To make the sauce:

Melt the butter or margarine in a large saucepan.

Stir in the flour and cook over a gentle heat for 2 minutes, but do not allow to brown.

Remove from the heat and stir in half of the liquid.

Return to the heat and stir the sauce briskly until it thickens.

Beat vigorously for a minute or two.

Stir in the rest of the liquid, bring to the boil and simmer for 3 minutes, beating vigorously.

Add the asparagus to the sauce and simmer for a further 5 minutes, stirring frequently to prevent burning.

Blend the sauce in a liquidizer, or put it through a sieve.

Stir in the lemon juice.

Season with salt and pepper.

Blend the cream with the egg yolks and add to the sauce.

Reheat, but do not allow to boil.

Just before serving, stir in the reserved asparagus tips.

WORCESTER SAUCE

In 1823 Lord Sandys, returning to Worcester from India, walked into the chemist shop owned by William Perrins and John Wheeley Lea with a recipe he had picked up during his time as Governor of Bengal. Lea and Perrins made up the sauce, with a few extra gallons for themselves. It tasted so horrible that they took the stone jars down to their cellar and forgot about them. Much later they found the jars, tasted the contents again, and realized that the sauce had matured and was now superb. In 1838 they started to manufacture it commercially, but were very careful to keep the essential ingredients and maturing time a secret. This recipe is for an inferior substitute.

1 pint (600 ml/ 2½ cups) brown malt vinegar
2 tablespoons anchovy essence
3 tablespoons walnut ketchup
2 tablespoons soy sauce
2 shallots, finely chopped
A pinch of salt

Mix all the ingredients together.

Put into a bottle and cork.

Shake the bottle twice a day for a fortnight.

Strain and bottle.

Use as required.

HEREFORD CIDER SAUCE

1 pint (600 ml/ 2½ cups) Hereford cider
¾ pint (450 ml/ 2 cups) brown sauce
1 bayleaf
2 cloves

To make the brown sauce:
1 small carrot
1 onion
1 oz (25 g) lard
1 oz (25 g) flour
¾ pint (450 ml/ 2 cups) stock
Salt and pepper

Thinly slice the carrot and onion.

Melt the lard in a saucepan and gently fry the carrot and onion until golden brown.

Stir in the flour and fry until it is also golden brown.

Stir in the stock.

Bring to the boil.

Season with salt and pepper.

Simmer for 30 minutes.

Strain the sauce and mix with the cider.

Add the bayleaf and cloves.

Bring to the boil again and simmer until the sauce is reduced to two-thirds.

Strain and serve.

CIDER CUP

Serves 6-8

2 pints (1.15 litres/ 5 cups) cider
Juice of half a lemon
3 tablespoons sugar
2 wineglasses brandy
1 wineglass Curacao
2 thin slices of lemon
A pinch of grated nutmeg
A sprig of borage

Mix all the ingredients in a punch bowl.

Add plenty of ice and the sprig of borage to garnish.

HOT CIDER PUNCH

4 pints (2.25 litres) cider
½ pint (300 ml/ 1¼ cups) rum
¼ pint (150 ml/ ⅔ cup) orange juice
2 tablespoons honey
4 whole allspice
6 cloves
2 cinnamon sticks

Put the cider, rum, orange juice, honey, allspice, cloves and one cinnamon stick into a large pan.

Heat thoroughly but do not allow to boil.

Warm a large punch bowl and break into it the remaining cinnamon stick.

Pour in the hot punch.

Serve immediately.

THE COUNTRY RECIPE SERIES

Available now @ £1.95 each

Cambridgeshire	Lancashire
Cornwall	Leicestershire
Cumberland & Westmorland	Norfolk
Derbyshire	Northumberland & Durham
Devon	Oxfordshire
Dorset	Somerset
Essex	Suffolk
Gloucestershire	Sussex
Hampshire	Warwickshire
Herefordshire & Worcestershire	Wiltshire
Kent	Yorkshire

Available @ £2.95 each:

Scottish Country Recipes
Welsh Country Recipes

All these books are available at your local bookshop or newsagent, or can be ordered direct from the publisher. Just tick the titles you require and fill in the form below. Prices and availability subject to change without notice.

Ravette Books Limited, 3 Glenside Estate, Star Road, Partridge Green, Horsham, West Sussex RH13 8RA.

Please send a cheque or postal order, and allow the following for postage and packing. UK 25p for one book and 10p for each additional book ordered.

Name ....

Address ....

....

....